YOUR STORY
MATTERS

An Anthology of Student Resiliency

Jennifer Liberty Clark
editor
Anoka Ramsey Community College

Kendall Hunt
publishing company

Cover Image © Shutterstock.com

Back Cover Image Courtesy of Anna-Jenae Clark

www.kendallhunt.com
Send all inquiries to:
4050 Westmark Drive
Dubuque, IA 52004-1840

Copyright © 2017 by Kendall Hunt Publishing Company

ISBN 978-1-5249-3718-8

Published in the United States of America

CONTENTS

PREFACE

A childhood friend once said that I was a "collector of people." I think a more accurate description is that "I'm a collector of people's stories." For as long as I can remember in my adult years I've been collecting the stories of people's lives. This is just the first time I've ever documented them. Earlier in my career, when I was teaching and working in the corporate sector, was really when the collection of stories began. I would hear the stories of my student's lives and they became a myriad of bundled inspiration within me. Some of their stories were heartbreaking, some were funny, and some were inspiring, but all led me to thoughts of hope and resiliency. Most of these students were professionals working in organizations around the metro area.

In 2004 I moved into higher education and I heard more stories, this time from students furthering their education and fulfilling their hopes and dreams. Through conversations with individual students and often through their writing assignments, I collected their stories each semester, tucking them away into the myriad of inspiration that has become an essential part of my spirit. These stories were similar to the ones I heard earlier in my career. Some were filled with heartbreak, some were funny, and many were very inspiring. They had a similar theme and that was again of HOPE and RESILIENCY. You see, if someone remains hopeful in the heartbreak of their individual circumstances, they might just find themselves sharing the details of those circumstances in a class or an instructor's office. They might even get to share them with the world. I feel humbled and honored that people have trusted me with their stories. In the case of, "Your Story Matters," they have trusted me enough to share their stories with you.

So, here we are in the summer of 2017 and I humbly am sharing with all of you only six of the stories that have come my way. This is a fraction [a tiny fraction] of the ones that remain in my mind. However, they are representative of many of the stories I've held close. They are stories of strength, of hope, of empowerment, of faith, and of resiliency.

These particular stories feature women, but I assure you that I have stories of men, too. Maybe there will be a part 2 of "Your Story Matters" featuring these men?

It is my hope that the stories of these six young women will inspire you like they have inspired me. Interwoven in the travesties of their experiences are strong, resilient women who are changing the world along their journey. So, thank you Bianca, Analise, Amanda, Tayder, Miranda, and Hunter. Thank you for trusting me and sharing your stories so that others may, too, be inspired to rise above the challenges that life throws their way.

Thank you, also, to the countless numbers of you who share your stories with others. It's the link to human connection and the place where empathy, love, and inclusivity are born. Also, thank you to Beth and Jennifer at Kendall Hunt Publishing for taking on this project and letting me share these stories. Finally, thank you to my daughter, Ahna-Jenae, for taking the pictures of these women and capturing their innermost beauty. You are another young woman who has inspired me with your resiliency and your hope. I get to live that journey with you because you are my daughter and for that I am blessed and forever grateful.

"And now these three remain:
faith, hope and love.
But the *greatest* of these is *love*."
Corinthians 13:13

FOREWORD

I have learned something from every teacher I have encountered, either as a student or as an educational leader. When I think about my time as a student, the best teachers were the ones who interspersed personal stories into larger conversations about the subject matter. The personal stories helped maintain interest, plus helped me to understand who they were as people, not just as the classroom leader. This ultimately helped me to grasp the relevance of what they were teaching to my own life, regardless of the subject. The teachers I struggled with were the ones who either forgot why they were passionate about the subject they were teaching or did not see a value in connecting the subject to the lives of their students. As an educational leader, I bring this same perspective into my interactions with college faculty members, ultimately confirming that expertise in a field does not equate to being a great teacher. A teacher can talk "at" students about what they know, but what truly sets an excellent teacher apart is two things, their willingness to be vulnerable and their willingness to listen. This book demonstrates how those two can intersect to create something special.

A teacher's willingness to be vulnerable is to acknowledge that they themselves are still learning, mistakes will be made, and they are human. This does not mean that standards are not set or held, instead students and teachers collaborate along the learning journey, with the goal to challenge students to achieve the standards while supporting them. To find this elusive balance of challenge and support, the teacher must first understand the starting point of their students. By sharing of themselves first, this encourages students to share pieces of themselves which sets the stage for the teacher to actively engage the student in a dialogue about how those life experiences relate to the content of the course. Ultimately helping students know they are cared for and accepted creates a classroom environment where students feel safe sharing who they are, their struggles, their successes, and their dreams. This environment provides opportunities for students to try out new ideas and opinions while engaging with different concepts to help them connect to their experiences in novel ways. By applying theory to these experiences, students have an opportunity to truly understand that the experiences are neither positive nor negative, it is their response to the experiences which makes them the unique individual they are today. What they may have once thought of as a burden or something that happened to them is something they can own and see as part of their journey to resiliency. It all begins with an excellent teacher who is willing to share their story and listen to the stories of others.

Each of the stories you will read in this anthology is unique to the individuals who shared them, but having a story is not unusual. All our students have stories, it just takes curiosity to ask about the story and a willingness to listen without judgment.

Deidra Peaslee, EdD

CHAPTER 1

STRIVING IN AMERICA: THE TALE OF AN AMERICAN HMONG GIRL

TAYDER YANG

Courtesy of Anna-Jenae Clark

It was hard to fit in to begin with. My parents came to America as immigrants in 1992 and as hard as it was for them to be in a different world, it is a struggle to adapt both cultures into my life. My name is Tayder Yang and I was born in Minneapolis, Minnesota. Growing up I've acquired some expectations that I needed to live up to, according to my culture. Why is it so hard?

A LITTLE HISTORY ON THE HMONG PEOPLE

The Hmong people did not have a land to be called their own. As tribal clans, they have migrated throughout Asia and now reside in different parts of the world such as America, Europe, and Australia just to name a few. Starting from ancient times, the emperor of China and the Hmong's king went into warfare. The Chinese wanted to conquer its neighboring people and the Hmong had to defend its land and people. The Hmong were outnumbered and therefore the Hmong had to surrender. Some would seek refuge in the Southeast Asia countries, some fled to the west into India and Europe, and the majority stayed behind to be taken over by China. The Hmong resided in Southeast Asia for centuries and one day a secret war took place alongside the Vietnam War. As communism was spreading to the Southeast Asia region, the CIA contracted the Hmong to assist in the war. Thousands were drafted including boys from 9 years old and above. Throughout the Vietnam War, many of the Hmong people fled into the jungles finding their way to Thailand. There were thousands of Hmong casualties including soldiers and civilians as a result of the secret war. Despite all, my grandparents made their way through the jungle, crossed the Mekong River, and took refuge in Thailand.

A LITTLE VILLAGE IN THAILAND

Imagine a small village known as a refugee camp in Thailand. It was called Ban Vinai. To grow up as a successful young man is to know how to build a house. Aside from this basic task, it is imperative to understand the religion known as Shamanism. Shamanism is the practice of spiritual sacrificing using animals such as a chicken, pig, or a cow. These animals are offered to the dead to gain luck and great health amongst the people. Keep in mind that not everyone is a Shaman but understanding it and seeking out Shamans is an important role of a successful young man to his family. One should seek marriage as young as 16. The reason is to acquire more labor force to assist his family needs such as farming and house chores as his parents are approaching their old age. The wife's purpose is to provide care for his parents and take over the responsibilities of his parent's farm. To grow up as a successful young woman, as early as 14 years of age essentially means marriage is upon her. She is to serve his parents and be there to assist them in every need.

GROWING UP IN AMERICA

Throughout my entire childhood, I was expected to know how to read, write, and speak Hmong. I was expected to do the exact opposite in school for English. It is hard to differentiate the language and grammar in English mainly because it is my second language. Living in the lifestyle back in Thailand, education had low access and was unaffordable so many families lived off of farming. My parents came to America with no educational history so it was hard for me to get the proper guidance I needed. I'd go to school to come back home and that was it. There was no talking about school nor talking about our day and it's ironic because it wasn't a rule. It just wasn't talked about so I never really felt like opening up to seek guidance from them. It also goes hand in hand with them not knowing or understanding English and because of this I didn't have a choice, but to do everything on my own.

Many students in America get the privilege to receive the extra guidance from their parents, especially in English. Having parents who understand the life here in America and the language is a clear advantage they may take for granted. I have to work twice as many steps and continually go the extra mile just to attain an average Hmong American lifestyle. It is mentally exhausting constantly seeking internal motivation because I am simply on my own; however, I am expected to live with my parents until marriage. A little ironic isn't it?

It's a little different in the Hmong culture than it is in the American culture when considering studying abroad or out of state. You're portrayed as a "bad girl" if you choose to study elsewhere besides home. The reason for this is unknown aside from safety; however, how am I expected to live my life if I can't even go out and explore? It feels like being locked up in a prison world without an actual physical appearance of a prison. Being a 19-year-old in the household of my father, I am not allowed to do what I want or make my own decisions. Of course this excludes day-to-day decisions or what I am going to eat. It's more than that. It's about who I am as my own person and how I want to spend my time as my own person. Being a Hmong girl means you are to stay with your parents until you are married. You can't move out under any circumstance because that just automatically means you must hate your parents and you are disobeying them. This is especially hard for me to live up to because I feel like moving out could be a good thing. It doesn't necessarily mean you are bad and you should be perceived as bad. To me, life is all about experiences and making mistakes but how can I do that when my hands are still held?

In today's society in America, equality of gender is preached; however, in the culture of Hmong starting from ancient ancestors, men are dominant and automatically have the authority over women. This ties back into juggling two different lifestyles and cultures because it takes a toll on how I feel about gender roles and equality. As time is evolving, younger generations within my culture are adapting to society's roles on gender but it is hard when parents don't participate in the same practice. It is frustrating when I get treated differently from my brothers simply because I am a girl. Things such as, going out to have fun with friends or even dress codes have guidelines I have to follow or I am considered "bad" or defiant. Women are to serve men and there is no refuting it because men will lose their manhood. Since my dad formed an authority bubble over him, as a little girl until now it is hard for me to talk to him about what's on my mind. Although I want to fight for what I believe in, I simply can't find the courage to express my feelings.

Oftentimes as I grew older in early adulthood, I never understood why some people wanted their parents to back off on their lives. I often hear them saying how tired they are of their parent's texting them while in college or always trying to interact with them to see how they're doing. It angers me in many ways because I only wish I could get that type of interaction with my own parents. I often compare my own life with theirs and I begin to feel nothing but envy. Emotional love from older generations isn't given for odd, unknown reasons. It impacts my lifestyle because I don't feel acknowledged. It affects the way I feel about my own life because I deserve that emotional support just like any other person does. It becomes an internal battle because anxiety forms from any foundation. Mine happens to be loneliness due to the lack of emotional support from my parents.

IMAGINING MY FUTURE

My intentions are to study Nutritional Science at a university after I finish my Associates of Arts degree at Anoka Ramsey Community College. The reason why I want to study nutritional science is because my culture does not eat the least bit healthy and I want to make a change to influence my own personal lifestyle as well as influence others. I am looking forward to the future because, of course, marriage and kids are on the timeline somewhere. Education is important to me and despite all the hardships I have gone through in school without my parents' help, my lifelong goal is to make sure I am there for my kids. When I say "there" I mean I am going to be there with my children and experience all of it, including the mental, physical, financial, and most importantly, the emotional aspects of life and love. It's important to me to be able to find the strength within myself and still find a way to pull through. Although it is still a struggle for me now, I hope that by sharing my message with others that they, too, can benefit by knowing that they aren't alone.

REFLECTION QUESTIONS

1. What do you think it has been like for Tayder to be the only English speaking person in her family?

2. Imagine where and how she might have to communicate on their behalf.

3. Are there situations in your life where you must advocate for others? Be specific.

4. How are young American women and young Hmong women different, based on the cultural aspects that Tayder spoke of?

CHAPTER 2

MY INVISIBLE BATTLE

Bianca Robison

Courtesy of Anna-Jenae Clark.

FEAR AT FIRST SIGHT

Life is supposed to be a challenge. We are all told during the tough periods in our lives, that we all have a purpose that must be fulfilled. It is important to find meaning, even when we feel there is no hope. My biggest challenge in life, to say the least, was not what I expected, when I first discovered it at age 3. It was a morning that did not begin like every day. I usually woke up and got out of bed to run through the hallway, and into the kitchen for breakfast. However, this particular morning was the start of the challenge I am currently facing, and it will continue for the rest of my life.

The reason for my awakening in bed was not from the voice of my mother, which it usually was. I overheard someone speaking over my head, so I opened my eyes. The figure standing at the foot of my bed looked like someone, or something that I had never seen before. He was all white, with eyes in his head, and he was wearing a top hat and a purple tuxedo. He was smiling, but he didn't say anything. I wanted to say hello but I stopped myself. He scared me. I knew what he was right away after observing him for a few minutes. When I realized that a walking, fancy, ghost-like skeleton was in my room, I wanted to tell someone. I sat up in bed and looked and looked at the open door to the living room. When I turned my head back to see my new ghost friend, he was not there.

As the typical 3-year-old that I was, I went on to the next thing which was to find my mom sitting on the sofa watching television.

"Mommy." I said calmly and reassuringly.

"Good morning, honey." She said very enthusiastically with a smile.

"Mommy." I repeated, this time with a sad frown.

"Bianca, what's wrong?"

I thought I would be giving her some bad news when I said, "There is a ghost in my room."

She laughed for a little while and then made me breakfast.

It is not unusual for children to have imaginary friends, which was my mother's initial thought. However, as I grew older, the figure in my room did not disappear. In fact, I began to see more things that no one else could. When I was five, they became stranger, and they impacted my behavior and emotions. My mother began to worry when I would run to her panicking. She took me to see a psychiatrist and I was diagnosed with an anxiety disorder that was to be treated with an antidepressant.

THE DIAGNOSIS

When I was eight, I could better describe the things that I was seeing, and was diagnosed with depression with psychotic symptoms, and was put on a mild antipsychotic medication. I had "flare-ups" every year during middle school and high school and frequently needed my medication adjusted. School was difficult, as I sometimes had trouble focusing. Even though I ate a well-balanced diet, and was a vegetarian, my medication had caused some weight gain. I was not very popular in middle school and became a victim of bullying. I refused to tell my peers that a medical condition was the reason for my appearance. My social life was not the best, but I thought it was more important for me to not experience any hallucinations. There were times when

I needed to be hospitalized because my mental illness interfered with my ability to function. I thought that my life would never change for the better, or that I could never be a contributing member of society. My perspective on life slowly began to change during my early teen years when I met a doctor who told me that he had schizophrenia. He helped me to believe that nothing is ever hopeless and that anything is possible. Psychotic disorders have a wide spectrum, and taking medication regularly helps to control the symptoms. During this time, a social worker referred me to a therapist who knew a great deal about mental illnesses.

Source: Bianca Robison

She is the same therapist that I continue to see on a weekly basis, and she encouraged me to find hobbies that can serve as a way to cope. I did not think that social activities would be helpful, but I became interested in theater in sixth grade and joined the school plays up until ninth grade. My favorite plays were the ones that were about fairy tales because they symbolized an alternative reality. Playing a green troll in sixth grade was the most memorable. Acting gave me a distraction, and it felt good to pretend that I was someone else. I also began learning German in middle school, which is where my family originated. Being able to communicate with my family from Germany over the phone felt like a huge accomplishment. In high school, I had more symptoms of anxiety, and I would choose to sit in a desk near the door in case that I needed to leave the classroom. Art classes were different.

ART AS THERAPY

I discovered that making a painting or a sculpture was a healthy way to express my emotions. I also took art classes outside of school at a place called Banfill-Locke Center for the Arts, and became a volunteer at age fifteen. My medium is watercolor with ink, and my creations are still sometimes displayed in their gallery. What people seem to enjoy most are the paintings that are inspired by the hallucinations that I had in the past. Since I graduated from high school, my illness became more manageable and this is mostly due to the right medication. As a graduation present, my mother and I spent a month in Germany.

We stayed in a village where she grew up. There are houses that were built in the 1700s and there are two castles within walking distance. It felt like being in a real-life fairytale and it also felt like home. I plan on moving to a town near Frankfurt at some point in my life. It is a peaceful country and I love their lifestyle. Before I move, I would like to finish my education and feel confident that I chose the right career path. College has greatly impacted my life and it also serves as a distraction.

THE STIGMA

During the more difficult times in my life, I did not believe that college would be a part of my future, and neither did most of my teachers in grade school. When I graduated from high school, some worried that I would not do well in college, but I made the Dean's list for my first two semesters. College gives me something to focus on and it feels good to know that I am doing something for myself. I plan to become a social worker to help people who are going through similar obstacles.

There is a huge stigma attached to mental illnesses. Some television shows portray people with schizophrenia or other psychotic disorders as very violent and dangerous individuals. Needless to say, crime shows greatly exaggerate my condition. They make people who are battling an illness into monsters, and I have trouble understanding why this is considered entertaining. Symptoms decrease when people take their medication as prescribed, and most are able to function and live a relatively normal life. For a very long time, I would avoid talking about any topic related to schizophrenia. The stigma created fear that I would behave violently, even though I consider myself to be a peaceful person. Some of my friendships have ended because I told them the label I was given.

In the past, there were times when my peers in middle school would see me speaking to a brick wall, and thought that I only wanted attention. I did not explain my condition to them because I knew it would make things worse, and I did not want them to know that I was living in two different worlds. Ignoring my hallucinations was difficult. Sometimes I would go months at a time when I needed my medication adjusted and during these times would have to keep telling myself that the hallucinations were not real. My condition has significantly improved as I entered adulthood and that is mostly due to my support team and finding medication that works.

I am very thankful that my condition was treated as soon as I experienced the harsh symptoms. My diagnosis was detected early, although symptoms typically surface at age 18. Doctors have told me that my case is unusual. Schizophrenia does not have a cure, but my doctors have told me that I came a long way and I should be proud for being a success story and should be looking forward to what I am yet to accomplish with my life.

MY PURPOSE

I have found purpose in helping others, as well as in my artwork. My paintings are a way to tell my life's story without using words. Drawing my hallucinations helped me cope and it felt good to know that I could create beauty from a nightmare. My paintings allow me to face my struggles and to change them into something more meaningful and creative. I would strongly recommend that people use art as a way to bring their inner feelings to the surface.

My plan for the future is to work with people who have mental health issues. As a social worker, I would play a huge role in finding the right resources for my clients. My treatment plan was created with the help of a social worker, and I think this career choice is a way to give back. I will arrange different therapies for my clients and will share with them what worked for me. Showing people that anyone is capable of anything can make a huge impact. When people feel hopeless, I want to tell them my story and to help them gain a better outlook on life. There are many stages in our lives as people, and although it is not always perfect, it gets better.

Source: Bianca Robison

REFLECTION QUESTIONS

1. What can you imagine early life as a child was like for Bianca? [Think about her hallucinations.]

2. What can you imagine being a bullied middle-schooler was like for her?

3. Have you ever been treated poorly for something that was "different" about you? Explain.

4. How do you think her love and talent for art helped her deal with her mental illness?

5. Do you have something that helps you to share your emotions and struggles? Describe it here.

CHAPTER 3

A JOURNEY OF SELF-ACCEPTANCE

Hunter Brokke

Courtesy of Anna-Jenae Clark.

My name is Hunter Brokke. I'm white, a lesbian, and this is a story of my journey with self-acceptance.

I was very young when I first realized that I was different from the rest of my peers. When I was in elementary school, around 4th or 5th grade, I would have dreams where I would be on a date with a girl. I would wake up and cry, wondering why I wasn't normal, why I wasn't having crushes on boys like my friends, why I wanted to hold hands with a girl instead of with a boy. This was very upsetting to me. So instead of trying to make sense of these feelings, I pushed them far back into my brain and forgot about them.

For years, I lived my life by going to school, sports practices, doing homework, and spending time with my friends. Dating was the last thing on my mind. By the time I was in 7th grade, I was starting to get the butterflies for a certain girl. To counteract those feelings, I started to date a boy. That "relationship" didn't last long. I had no greater feeling for him other than friendship. I didn't think he was cute in *that* way, I didn't like him in *that* way, and I didn't want to hug him. That was all the criteria you needed to have in order to be labeled boyfriend/girlfriend in middle school.

I think at this point it would be a good time to tell you about my family's opinion on the LGBTQ community. My mom and dad were not kind when sharing their thoughts on the matter. They would say things like, "why do they have to be so flamboyant/butch?", "why do they have to hold hands in public?", "if a girl is a lesbian why is she attracted to someone who looks like a man?" My parents were disgusted by gay people. They believed that being gay was a choice and that it was a wrong one. My younger brother hadn't told me his opinion on it, mostly because he probably knew little about it. Then there is my aunt. She is about 10 years younger than my parents and her views of gay people were completely different. My aunt is a very accepting person, but I still did not feel comfortable enough to confide in her because I felt like it would be unsafe. On top of all of this I still didn't accept myself as a gay person. I would tell myself that this was just a phase or that I am not trying hard enough when it came to liking boys.

At this point, not only am I going through the struggles of being a girl in middle school, I now am worried that if I am gay, I will not be accepted by my own family. This made me feel very alone which led to constant stress and anxiety, which led to depression. I had no one to talk to, no healthy outlet for what was causing me so much pain on the inside. So, I ultimately turned to self-harm. I would numb my feelings or push them to the back of my head to try to deal with them. The girl that I was talking to would help a little when I would get bad again. She would help distract me from the dark thoughts. After a few months of getting to know her I got the butterflies again and we started dating. She was my first girlfriend. At the time, I was halfway through 8th grade.

This relationship wasn't the healthiest, but I didn't know any better. I thought that someone who was controlling must care a lot about me. She was the only person that I could talk to about who I truly was. I still wasn't accepting myself but I was trying to work through it. I didn't think I could confide in my friends because I didn't think they would accept me. I knew I couldn't tell my parents. Being able to talk to someone who understood how I was feeling helped to start lifting the weight that was dragging me down. Because of this inner conflict, I would get so worked up at the thought of being a full-blown lesbian, so to calm myself I would think, "Oh it's OK, you're just questioning. When you grow up, you'll have a husband, children, and a nice *normal* life." This was my way of pushing my true identity away.

A few months later my mom went through my phone. She saw the text messages between my girlfriend and I. It was absolutely catastrophic. She was yelling and screaming, saying that she could not have a gay as a daughter. All I could do was cry and lie. To pacify her I told her that this was all just a prank. I claimed that I wasn't gay and that this was all just a joke. After hours of lying through my teeth, she finally believed me. This is what shattered any last hope that my mother would accept me for who I was. So, I started to distance myself from my family and friends. I felt like an imposter. None of them knew the real me. I also ended my relationship to try and prove to myself that I wasn't gay. I became isolated, numb, and even more depressed.

Again, I buried myself in school, sports, and now I could work. I never gave myself any free time because if I did I would start to think deeper than surface level. The beginning of my sophomore year in high school I met another girl. I fell for her fast. We started dating and halfway through my 10th grade year, I came out of the closet to my friends. All three accepted me with love and open arms, which helped me more than they could ever know. This was my first step in the direction of self-acceptance.

Even though I was slowly starting to become OK with who I was, I still wanted to be what I thought was normal. Some days were worse than others and I would turn to alcohol to help me cope. This didn't happen often, only when I had nothing to keep my mind occupied and only when I was alone.

This continued for one more year. My girlfriend and I had just celebrated our first anniversary a few months back and I started to think about coming out to my family.

For months I went back and forth on whether I should or should not tell my parents. The reaction from my mother three years earlier was still cemented into my memory. I was terrified of being disowned and kicked out of the house. At the time I was 17 years old and the thought of not having a place to live would give me nightmares.

Finally, on Saturday, June 14, 2014, I decided that I was going to come out to my parents. My family and I were at our camper for the weekend. I had been contemplating all day on if I should tell them or not. After hours of stress I got the courage to tell my mom. This was after we had dinner, so she was in the camper washing the dishes. I walked in, closed the door, and sat on the couch. I sat there for about 20 minutes making small talk and feeling sick to my stomach. Eventually I blurted out, "I need to tell you something!" My heart was pounding and I immediately felt like I had made a huge mistake. My mom jumped to conclusions and asked if I was pregnant. I laughed nervously and said, "No, I'm gay," then I just started bawling. She said that everything is OK and that she loves me unconditionally. This was not the reaction that I was expecting. We stayed in the camper for an hour while I was calming down and we talked. The next day I told my dad. I was truly shocked by their reactions. I expected something along the lines of screaming and unacceptance. The weight that had been lifted off my shoulders was indescribable.

Being able to show my family the real me has been one of the most joyful times in my life. Looking back now at my struggle I have no idea what got me through it. The only support system that I had were my two close friends, my brother, and my girlfriend. I believe what kept me going was their support, my hope that things would eventually get better, and my stubbornness. My aunt also helped without me knowing. Starting four years before I came out to my parents, she would continuously talk to them about how they need to just accept me, that I am the same person, that I am still their daughter. I could never thank her enough. It was like she knew and was smoothing the path for me.

Today I am 20 years old. This June will mark three years of being "out" to my family. To be honest I am much happier and healthier than at any other point in my life. I currently work full-time and go to school at Anoka Ramsey Community College. I am with a woman that I am madly in love with and we have been together for almost two years. I am close with my entire family and spend time with them often. I have decided to pursue a degree in psychology with one of the career paths being a therapist for LGBTQ+ youth.

In the future, I hope to hold a career that I can be proud of, own a decent home, be married, and start a family. Really these are no different from most people's dreams of their future. My best advice that I could give to anyone who feels different and is struggling with who they really are is that you just need to embrace yourself as you are. Once you accept yourself, the weight of having to hide your whole life is lifted from your shoulders and you will be much, much happier.

REFLECTION QUESTIONS

1. What can you imagine life as a child and middle-schooler was like for Hunter repressing her true identity?

2. Are there parts of yourself that you hide? (Think broadly: personality characteristic, bad habit, other.)

3. Have you ever then later revealed that part of yourself and then been accepted by others the way Hunter was accepted by her family?

4. In what ways has she made herself vulnerable? Be specific.

5. How might you make yourself more vulnerable?

CHAPTER 4

ROLL WITH IT

Analise Tellez

Courtesy of Anna-Jenae Clark.

My name is Analise Tellez. I was born April 9, 1992, at North Memorial Hospital. When I was born there were some complications due to Group B Strep. As a result, I suffered brain damage to the back left side of my brain and almost died. The brain damage I received caused me to have Spastic Quadriplegic Cerebral Palsy and Ataxia. Cerebral Palsy affects the way I move. I can walk but I need a wheelchair for long distances. Ataxia affects my movement, so I sometimes shake uncontrollably as I try to move my arms for certain tasks. When I was a child I went to the Courage Center a few times a week for physical, occupational, and speech therapy. My arms started to hurt in kindergarten. They began to hurt more and more each day. As each day came the pain would get worse until I couldn't move them. This would last a few weeks and stop for a while then it would start up again. My doctors really don't have an answer for why this happens. Every six months I have Botox and Phenol block injections in my arms, legs, and feet. These treatments help relax my muscles so I can move easier and have less pain. Cerebral Palsy causes my muscles to tighten up. I also have a learning disability. I do not read at the same level a person my age would. I can learn but it takes me longer than it would take the average person. My handwriting is awful because I can't control my muscles smoothly like the average person can, most people can't read my writing.

I was in special education from elementary throughout high school. In elementary school I was in the regular classroom for part of the day and then I would go work with the best special education teacher I could ever ask for. This particular teacher would work on reading and math with me. When I was in the first grade I had a major surgery on 07-06-99. The surgical intervention performed would include bilateral femoral valgus derotational osteotomies, bilateral rectus femoris to gracilis transfers, bilateral gastrocnemius recession, and bilateral calcaneus lengthening procedures were all formulated as part of the most appropriate surgical plan. In simple language, they cut my femurs and rotated them slightly, they re-located some tendons on my knees, they lengthened the tendons on my calves, and I had surgery on my ankles. The goal of these surgeries was to improve my stance phase stability, improve knee alignment and flexion, and improve the alignment of the feet so as to decrease the functional demands of the brace, and hopefully to decrease my O2 consumption and decrease the work of walking. I was in the hospital for about five days. I was out school for an extended period of time, but my special education teacher went above and beyond and actually came to my house. She did the lessons with me, so I wouldn't fall behind. She did not have to do this and take time out of her day, but she did. This teacher truly cared, not just about me but about all her students as well.

When middle school came along it was a little different. I always got along with my peers, but I did have one teacher who was mean to me. I was in a special education English class and we were brainstorming about a paper we had to write. The topic was what are your plans after high school? I explained to him that I didn't know exactly what I wanted to do but most likely go to college. My teacher stated, "Analise, between your handwriting and your mental capacity you might want to rethink this. This is an unlikely goal." I did believe him for a long time because he was a teacher. I figured he knew what he was talking about. High school went well for me. I was put into regular education classes except for reading and math. I still had struggles and I relied on paraprofessionals. I graduated with honors from Anoka High School in 2010. I forgot all about going to college because I did not feel it was realistic. After high school I attended a transitional program through the Anoka Hennepin School District for people with disabilities. The program was called Transitions Plus for young adults 18 to 21 years of age. The main focus of this school is to help people with disabilities have a normal life like everyone else. They helped me with simple everyday things like balancing a checkbook, looking for apartments, creating a resume, and finding a job. My best friend worked at a local grocery store as a sample lady. She informed me they were hiring and I should apply. The staff at the Transitions Plus program helped me apply and I got my interview. The employer loved me on the phone but when she saw me roll in I could tell she was disappointed. The first thing she said to me was "Can you even walk?" I explained to her that I can but it's difficult for me. She replied "If you can't stand for six hours straight this is not the job for you," and she turned around and walked away. I did know that there were (and still are) employees of this company that are allowed to sit on stools as they work. My interview lasted less than five minutes. I felt horrible about this. I thought in this day and age people were more accepting of others. This is the point in my life when I found out I was wrong. This was tough for me and is still hard for me to this day. I moved on and the teachers who worked at Transitions Plus encouraged me to try to take an intro to college class at Anoka Ramsey and see if I was able to succeed. I loved it. My final year at Transitions Plus they allowed me to take a few developmental classes at the community college for part of the day and take their classes the other half of the day. The developmental classes I took at ARCC had a significant role in helping me achieve my college goals. I enjoyed ARCC so much I decided to attempt to get a degree. The Transitions Plus staff are the reason why I started my college journey. They had faith in me and told me it was possible. It felt wonderful that they cared so much about me.

I am currently a student at Anoka Ramsey Community College and plan to graduate in the fall of 2017 with my Associate degree in Arts and Science. I would like to do something in social services and help people the way others have helped me. School is still a struggle for me, but I have a wonderful support system. Disability services at ARCC play a big role in my college life. They do everything possible, so I have every opportunity to be successful like a typical student. My family and friends help and encourage me on a daily basis. They have stuck by me through thick and thin. Without them I would not be where I am today. My mom is one of the biggest support systems I have. She drives me back and forth to school and appointments. She is also there to help me with homework, so I understand the information. If I did not have her, college would not be possible for me. When my mom cannot make me understand something like science my brother takes over. He will explain it to me in several different ways until it clicks. At times he does get frustrated with me and says things like "talking to you is like talking to a lamp." Frustrated or not, he continues to study with me.

Job opportunities continue to be an issue with me because it is hard for me to show employers that I am more than capable of doing the job. After I roll in they usually take one look at me and say "goodbye." I love to work out and try to stay in shape. My mom refers to me as a "gym rat." I work out on my own and with my dad. I no longer have to go to the Courage Center for therapy. My doctor encourages me to keep working out in the gym and staying as active as possible. I still have my injections every six months. The pain in my arms is ongoing but it is just part of my life. My friends and I enjoy going to parties, attending concerts, and of course shopping. My friends don't seem to mind or be affected by my disability. They just come over and pick me up and then we are off. When I'm with them I feel perfectly normal. I feel like having a disability makes it easier to figure out who your true friends are. They do make fun of me every chance they get, but I could not imagine my life without them. I am blessed to have so many positive people in my life. I did make a huge improvement with my reading (thanks to a developmental reading class), but I am still not at the level I know I should be at. My lovely handwriting remains the same. It is very frustrating for me because at times I can't even read it. This will never improve, so I have a feeling this will be a life-long struggle. I am happy to say there are many programs available to help with these struggles. I use Dragon, a speech recognition program, and my favorite is Co-Writer, a word prediction program that helps me type and write. I will do my best to not let this problem get in my way.

When I think about my future like most people, it does scare me. I imagine myself having a positive impact on society. My goal in the near future is to go skydiving. I think it would be amazing and it would make me feel so free. I absolutely want to travel the world and experience different cultures while I am still young. I love people and would like to learn as much as I can about people, their beliefs, and their lifestyles. I would love to have the typical American dream lifestyle. I would hope to have a good job, a husband, a few kids, and a dog. I am not sure where I would live, but I think it would be cool to move out of state, since I have lived in Minnesota my whole life. Everyone has their own issues. I understand my life is not going to be an easy ride but I will do my best to be the best person I can be. There is no such thing as the perfect life. If I had a choice I would not have my disability, but then I think it is part of me. It might not be the stereotypical "perfect life" everyone wants, but it's my life. I can honestly say I would not change it for the world. This is me and I am ready to put myself out there and see where life takes me.

REFLECTION QUESTIONS

1. What can you imagine life as a child was like for Analise? Think about it from a physical as well as emotional and psychological aspects.

2. How do you think Analise's optimistic outlook has impacted her physical challenges?

3. How might this same optimism help her in her future endeavors? Be specific.

4. When has optimism "won" in your life? Be specific.

CHAPTER 5

LOVE NEVER FAILS

Amanda Johnson

© theromb/Shutterstock.com

Due to the sensitivity of the topics discussed, the names have been changed to protect the privacy of the individuals within this story.

THE PAST

I can't remember when it "started" but the farthest back that I remember is when my mom, sister, and I lived in a duplex. Back then I was probably 8 years old and my sister was 12 years old. We shared a bed but I never minded. I idolized her and everything she did. My mom had just started seeing Steve, whom she would have my three younger brothers with. On the other side of the duplex lived my mom's best friend Tina, her husband, daughter, and son. I remember always going over to Tina's place. Her daughter, Alicia, was the same age as my sister and they would often spend time together without me. I don't remember feeling left out. I've always liked to spend time by myself.

One night my mom got me up saying that there was a fire at Tina's place. I remember being outside with my training bra on and a warm blanket. One time I remember being in Alicia's room. She never let me in her room. We sat on the floor beside her bed and she kissed me and told me to do inappropriate things to her. I didn't know it was wrong. She told me not to tell anyone or I would get in trouble. I never did. Back at home things were getting intense with my mom and sister. I tried to stay out of it but I couldn't seem to ignore the yelling and screaming. My sister would tell me things that mom was doing to her like kicking her and beating her with the spatula. She would run away often and told me that we could live in a better home, I just had to let her hit me and make bruises on me so we would never have to live with mom ever again. At this time, my mom had given birth to my oldest younger brother and she was pregnant again with my second brother. My mom and sister were still fighting at home whenever my sister was there.

One time my mom went to go find where my sister was and I remember Steve came back and told me that mom was in the hospital because my sister kicked her in the stomach. My sister didn't come home anymore. But she would write me letters about how much she missed me. My mom delivered my second brother and decided she was "done with this county" so we moved to another town. Things seemed like they were getting better without my sister but I never felt comfortable with Steve. I remember times that I would be changing in my room or showering and he would peek in. I never told mom because I thought she wouldn't believe me. I was also getting bullied in school. I hated lunchtime the most in 5th–6th grade because no one wanted to sit with me. In one of my classes in 5th grade a girl didn't want my desk beside hers so she tipped my desk over and everything came out. I went to lunch that day and made a motion like I was going to shoot myself in the head and someone told my homeroom teacher. He pulled me out of lunch and yelled at me about making actions like that in front of other students. Whenever I got home from school I would go in my room and look at my ceiling hoping that it would crush me.

During this time I was also starting to have issues at home with mom. She was trying to have a baby and I remember one time specifically that she miscarried. She told me that it was all the stress that I caused her that made her miscarry. I've always wanted a little sister and I sometimes wonder if I might have had one if I didn't make my mom so stressed out. We always argued and because I didn't have friends at school she was my only friend. We started having a therapist come in (who I still go to see 9 years later) and things looked like they were getting better. Then we moved to a different town. I was in the middle of 6th grade and I was really starting to make some friends. But my grades fell. Mom was not having it. She pulled me out of public school and I started online school. Steve and my mom were fighting a lot and so were my mom and I. She would punish me for whatever I did wrong by taking away everything—clothes, belongings, anything, and she would throw them away. But I loved her so much. We would sit up in her room and watch *Buffy The Vampire Slayer*, and she would tell me whatever was on her mind and vice versa. But the fighting was getting worse. In my mind, I always thought that if you did something wrong there was supposed to be a punishment and that may or may not be physical. But it was always very physical. And, in all honesty, I could get over that. It was the words that she would tell me that still hurt to this day.

Mom sent me down to Iowa to live with my cousins when I was 12 because she wanted me to understand how good I had it at home and how grateful I should be. I was almost certain they hated me and I felt so alone. I called my mom almost every night to apologize for what I did to her and how I wanted to come home. After one month, she let me come home on a bus and things were okay. For a few weeks, anyway. She had my youngest brother and started going out more. She started working as a DJ and more often than not she wouldn't come home. My brothers were 5, 4, and maybe 1 year old at the time. I would have to take care of all three boys when mom was gone, sometimes days at a time. I took care of my youngest brother so carefully that whenever he fell asleep in my arms I was afraid to lay him down by himself because I didn't want him to cry and me not be there. I was 13. At that time, I was still online schooled and I hated it but mom wasn't going to change her mind. I never went outside and my hours were messed up. I would go to sleep when the sun came up and wake up at sundown. The computer that I did my homework on had every other website blocked and all the television channels were blocked. I listened to the radio a lot until mom took that away, too. I wasn't eating very much and whatever I did eat, I threw up right away. Mom found me in the bathroom one time and got very upset, she told me she didn't want to find me doing that again. I started cutting, too. But not because it made me feel better or gave me relief, but it made me feel SOMETHING. I could control that part of my life.

The fighting was getting so bad that I tried seeing if my cousins would let me live with them again. Mom must have not wanted me to go. The day that I left she told me that she didn't care if I left or died. I will never forget that. I try to rationalize a lot of the things that my mom said or did but that one still sits with me. The worst part of leaving was that I was going to miss my brothers. Mom said she would make sure that they wouldn't remember me. My paternal grandparents drove me all the way down to Iowa. My cousin enrolled me in public school and a week later when my mom somehow found out, she drove down to my cousin's house and had me get my things to go back home with her. When I got back home I was really starting to feel like I hit rock bottom. But at that point I felt comfortable. I felt like I had reached the lowest point and there was nothing that mom could do or say to make me feel worse. But at the same time, she was still my best friend and I loved her so much. I never thought that she did anything wrong at the time because she was just punishing me for whatever I did wrong. I was the problem.

At some point when I was 13 mom wanted me to take an antidepressant. I tried to explain to her that I didn't want to feel happy and I was okay where I was. My logic was that if I started taking antidepressants that I would feel those highs and lows and I didn't want that. It was much easier to feel low all the time. My mom did not like when I disobeyed her so when she had the pill for me to take and I refused she took me to the police department to see if they would do anything about it. They told mom to bring me to the hospital. During the whole car ride to Children's Hospital, I can't remember what she said to me. But I know that she was talking the whole time. It was snowing outside that night and I remember wishing that the car would crash but that mom would be safe. I stayed on the inpatient unit for two weeks. Most of the adolescents were there for three to five days. They decided to put me on a 72-hour hold to keep mom from taking me home. But the only way they could do that was to put me on the locked part of the unit. I had to get completely undressed as they made sure I did not have any weapons or objects on me. I remember thinking it wasn't fair. I wanted to go home. I wasn't some psycho that couldn't be trusted. I stayed on the locked unit of the hospital for one more week. I could tell the staff was starting to feel bad for me as the nurses would come into my room and spend a lot of time with me. I would be escorted to court to sit and hear how my mom can't take me blah blah blah and they needed more time to find a place for me. Then I would be escorted back to the hospital. It was hell. I just wanted to go home.

After three weeks in the hospital I was placed in a foster home on February 28th, 2012. That of which I stayed at for the next 4 1/2 years. The court dates were always the worst. I don't know why I feared the judge as much as I did. I had a lawyer that represented me, but I could never look him in the eye whenever we spoke. I'm still not very sure what he looked like, but he had very nice shoes. My paternal grandparents always tried to make it to the court dates and they would drag along my father with them. He's never tried to initiate a relationship with me until I was placed in foster care. I think my mom always knew how much that hurt me.

Anyway, sometimes my sister would come to the court dates as well. It was like all my family members came out of their hiding places to "support" me. It felt more like they were against mom. Just thinking back to how she would sit on the other side of the courtroom by herself hurts me so much. She's my mom and even more my best friend, and I felt so guilty that I was the one that did this to her. We only had each other. My mom has always appeared strong and confident to me. She had the prettiest dark skin and the most outgoing personality. She would strike up conversations with strangers at stores and maintain relationships with them. That just amazes me. She has a trademark gap in-between her teeth and I would secretly wish I had one just like her. When I saw her in court it was a different mom. She looked alone and scared. We wouldn't talk to each other outside of court but occasionally she would come up to me afterward and ask, "Are you serious Amanda?" I can still hear the way her voice cracked when she asked me that.

Eventually the court came to the decision in early June 2012 that my mom would take me back home. By that time, I had grown a relationship with my foster family and I was devastated that I had to go home. It was a nightmare. I was finally starting to love my life and see a future for myself. I went home in early June and was back in the hospital and foster care by August. Just in time to start my sophomore year of high school at a public school. It was very difficult for me still at my foster home. I would cover all the mirrors in my room because I couldn't look at myself and I slept on the floor of my closet because I didn't think I deserved to sleep in my bed. I argued with my foster parents daily and would stay in my room all the time. It took a very long time for me to trust both of my foster-parents, but our relationship grew and they have shown me that I can trust them as my parents.

THE PRESENT

Today I am 19 years old. I moved out of my foster home into my own apartment. I still maintain a good relationship with my foster family. I have a great work ethic and am working on paying off my second new car. I went to school for my LPN and I am currently working as a nurse. I love my job and I work with a fantastic group of nurses although there are some nursing assistants that have been trying to disrespect me and treat me poorly. I cry sometimes when I drive home. I was accepted into the RN program here at Anoka Ramsey and I will graduate with my BSN the spring before my 23rd birthday. Everyone around me is so proud of me and how far I have come. I can tell that most people would think that I have my whole life together and that I have overcome my past. I constantly feel guilty that I never spend time with them, but I use school and work as an excuse because I am afraid that if I spend time with them they will see through my happy façade.

I make a lot of money for someone my age and I am living very comfortably, but I'm starting to learn that money and even success cannot make you happy. I live by myself but I can't be comfortable alone and often have people over to distract me. I have been seeing the same therapist for 9 years and I think that everyone should have someone who is paid to talk to you. For real. Except at this point we are both comfortable with each other and Angie will talk about her problems with me. I don't want to sound ungrateful, but sometimes I don't care. I deal with ADHD and anxiety and although I have always been against pills to help me with some of my problems (kind of ironic as a nurse), I have started taking medication to help me with my depression.

I am working on my self-esteem but most of the time I am very self-conscious and do not feel comfortable in my body. I know that guys like the way that I look so I use that to make me feel somewhat happy with myself. It never lasts and then like every other girl I wonder, "Why so and so never called me back?" You would think that I would catch on at some point.

My mom is getting more comfortable with me and will let me see my little brothers from time to time. The first time I saw my youngest brother after I left home was when he was 4 years old. He had no idea who I was. That still kills me sometimes. I try to overcompensate by investing more time with him than I do with the other boys. My sister is declining. She isn't the older sister that I remember her being. The last time I saw her a few weeks ago, I was speechless. She is a shell of who she used to be. She is using drugs and had her two babies taken away from her. They are both in foster care now. It feels like a sick joke. The county is requesting that I care for the older of her two children. Her son is 2 years old. I need to decide if I can take guardianship of him or he will stay in foster care indefinitely. I am working and going to school full-time. Everyone is telling me that it's a bad idea to take care of him and how I need to focus on myself right now. But that isn't fair to him. I can't sleep at night and I'm afraid of making the wrong decision.

When I think about my past . . . I don't. I do not think about it in all honesty. The experiences, though they have helped me become the resilient young woman that I am today, still bring up a lot of unpleasant emotions, memories, and questions. I am still learning to forgive myself and my mother for what has happened in my life. And although most people would say that it wasn't my fault I know that I still hurt my mother. When people ask me if I was abused as a child, I either find myself saying "no" because I do not want them to think I am some victim of a horrible childhood trauma or I'll say "yes" and feel like a liar because I don't feel like my mom was really trying to hurt me. But as I think about my past at this moment, I realize that I am stronger than I thought I was. I met a lot of children and teens that were in much worse situations than I so I learned how to be grateful for my situation. My past has allowed me to mature very quickly and makes me very thankful for the life that I have now. I am learning that it is okay for me to be "selfish," that is, take care of my own needs right now and ask for help when I need it. I have learned from my past that all people are fragile and need to be cared for and loved. Because love is what saves people. Love is what saved me. Specifically the love and support that I received from my family and friends. When I knew that I was valued by others, I wanted to live and be successful for them. By doing so, I learned that I have value regardless of how dark my past was.

THE FUTURE

It's very strange to think about my future because I did not think that I would make it this long. Now I'm just planning along the way. In the future, I want to be happy with myself and love myself the way so many others love me. I hope in the future that I can support my family. When I was younger I would tell my mom that she could live in the basement of my mansion and I would take care of her. I want to raise more awareness about child abuse and once I finish nursing school I would like to work with children and adolescents in psychiatric care. I don't know if it will ever change for me in the future but I don't see myself having children. I am afraid that I will treat them the way my mom treated me and I would never forgive myself. I want to travel and see the world. Initially after graduating with my BSN I intend to start working as a travel nurse around the US and beyond. I want to leave this earth knowing that I loved and cared for everyone I met. I've got a long way to go but first I need to start by loving me.

REFLECTION QUESTIONS

1. What can you imagine life as a child was like for Amanda?

2. What role does "childhood attachment" play in her story?

3. How might she use the travesty of childhood abuse to help her in the future to push through other life challenges? Be specific.

4. Name a time in your own life that you had to rise above being treated badly. Be as specific as possible.

CHAPTER 6

CANCER DOES NOT DEFINE ME

Miranda Mead

Courtesy of Anna-Jenae Clark.

On December 1, 2015, just days after my 16th birthday, I was diagnosed with a stage four bone cancer called Ewing's Sarcoma. I was given a 30% chance of survival as the cancer had metastasized from my sacrum to my lungs. I underwent 14 rounds of chemotherapy, 31 days of proton radiation, multiple surgeries, and lastly 10 days of radiation on my lungs at the very end of treatment. I am a cancer survivor.

It took about six months to diagnose my cancer. Ewing Sarcoma typically takes six to nine months to diagnose. I had been fighting back pain for over six months. I was visiting a chiropractor three times a week over my lunch break. I was a huge cross country runner who ran over eight miles a day. I thought I had pulled something in my back and that was the reason why my back always hurt. I never imagined that I had a six-inch tumor consuming my sacrum.

Daily I was consuming roughly 12 pills of ibuprofen and crashing around 7:30 every night because the pain was just too much. What really threw me off, though, was when I went to itch my left hamstring and I couldn't feel my fingers on my hamstring. I also had been constipated over two weeks and I was starting to lose control over my bowel and bladder. Hearing all these symptoms my chiropractor recommended an MRI at once. The MRI technicians were very nice to me, too nice. I can clearly remember one lady telling me I could have two snacks instead of just one. At the very end while I was leaving she turned and spoke rather softly and said, "Have a great Thanksgiving! And good luck . . ." I sat there in the car and pondered aloud to my mom, "Good luck?" I questioned. Why the heck would she tell me good luck? That seemed very unsettling. After my MRI appointment I was scheduled to go see a neurologist to figure out why my entire left leg was numb. While at the neurologist my mom received a phone call that forever changed both our lives. Since my situation was so dire, the radiologist read the MRI and called back with the results. The radiologist told my mom about the six-inch tumor found at the bottom of my spine.

I left immediately from the neurologist's office and went straight to a children's hospital where I spent the next three weeks in the intensive care unit—a living hell. I truly do not recall much from PICU, the pediatric intensive care unit, as I was on so many drugs, but I have been able to put together what actually happened from stories told by friends and family.

I was misdiagnosed when I first went in PICU. The doctors told me I did not have cancer. The doctors diagnosed me with some rare form of bone cyst. The oncologist had not had time to weigh in on my scans. She knew it was cancer when she saw the scans.

From December 1 to December 4 I was under sedation while the doctors performed multiple tests and procedures to confirm my diagnosis. During those three days the doctors molecularly confirmed my diagnosis of Ewing's Sarcoma. Shortly after the anesthesia wore off I was given a pain medication called ketamine. I hallucinated for 36 hours. The hallucinations started innocent and turned more sinister as the night wore on. These hallucinations still haunt my nightmares. It started with harmless drumming, a simple timpani echoing in the hallway. I soon started to hear voices coming from the corner of my room. These voices were not speaking English. It seemed to be gibberish, an incantation some cult would have murmured. I started to hear voices trying to summon the devil, that's when I began to see shadows reaching into me. Most of the shadows were dark and evil. I did my best to block out the vile shadows and let in the pure, light ones. I remember holding my nurse's hand saying "The Lord's Prayer" aloud together while I struggled to fight the shadows. For 36 hours I fought the demons until the effects wore off. I refused to sleep the next few nights.

People always ask me what the hardest part of my treatment was. I always flash back to that night and consider telling them this horrific experience; however, that was only one night. I think about telling people how many times I puked, my record being five times in one day. Maybe I would mention the awful side effects from radiation which consisted of a third degree burn and permanent bone damage. Perhaps I could mention the long-term side effects of chemotherapy and how it has been almost one year since the end of my treatment and I still can't run, or how I consider myself a human pin cushion because I have received over 600 needle pokes. But I always say, the hardest part of my treatment, by far, has been the emotional damage.

No longer am I a normal teenager pacing the high school hallways. The truth of the matter is that I am a high school student who has been through one hell of a battle. I had to fight to live, something many high school aged kids struggle to comprehend. I deal with PTSD and panic attacks because of my experiences.

Through this experience, I recognized the true value of friendship. One friend went above and beyond and truly stayed by my side throughout everything. She and I have become so close throughout this journey. She would often miss school and spend her days at the hospital, she would drive down to the clinic with me, and lastly, she was always there if I needed something. I could not have beat cancer without the endless support of her and her family.

During treatment I started volunteering with a national organization called The Truth 365. They provided me with a platform to speak my mind and talk about how childhood cancer has affected my life. I was given a voice. So many times during my treatment I had no choices, volunteering on behalf of this organization gave me choices. I have done public service announcements, spoken on Wall Street, participated in photo shoots to raise awareness for childhood cancer, and I have hosted an event on the National Mall called Curefest. My volunteer service led me to win a national award called the Prudential Spirit of Community Award. I received a $1,000 scholarship and an all expense paid trip to D.C. I plan to continue my volunteer efforts to make a difference in the childhood cancer community.

Currently I am cancer free! I have gotten a tattoo symbolizing strength and positivity constantly reminding me how strong I am. I have dreams of being the runner I once was. I plan to go into radiation therapy and help other children fight cancer the way my team at the clinic helped me. I am beyond thankful to be alive today. The main thing I learned from my entire journey is to appreciate the little things in life. A lot of times people, teenagers especially, tend to overlook the simple things and take life for granted. I have learned to embrace every moment and that is definitely something I would love to teach others how to do. It is vital to live in the present moment and not worry about what the future holds, but rather embrace the now and live life to the absolute fullest.

REFLECTION QUESTIONS

1. What can you imagine receiving news of her cancer diagnosis was like for Miranda?

2. What did she lose through her cancer fight? What did she gain?

3. What type of news have you received in your lifetime that has caused you some level of devastation? Please describe it, specifically.

4. What has come from this cancer diagnosis that is positive in Miranda's life?

5. How do you think that Miranda's relationships were affected by her cancer? Think about her parents, brother, and close friends? What challenges would there be for them and her?

CHAPTER 7

RESILIENCY

Courtesy of Anna-Jenae Clark.

Psychology Today defines resilience as,

> "that ineffable quality that allows some people to be knocked down by life and come back stronger than ever. Rather than letting failure overcome them and drain their resolve, they find a way to rise from the ashes. Psychologists have identified some of the factors that make someone resilient, among them a positive attitude, optimism, the ability to regulate emotions, and the ability to see failure as a form of helpful feedback. Even after misfortune, resilient people are blessed with such an outlook that they are able to change course and soldier on" [Sussex Publishers].

According to the Bureau of Public Affairs,

> "resilience refers to the ability to successfully adapt to stressors, maintaining psychological well-being in the face of adversity. It's the ability to 'bounce back' from difficult experiences. Resilience is not a trait that people either have or don't have. It involves behaviors, thoughts, and actions that can be learned and developed in everyone."

All of our stories have elements of facing some type of adversity. **Hunter** struggled with the self-acceptance because of her sexual orientation. **Analise** has had many physical challenges due to her cerebral palsy. **Bianca** struggled with both the identification and treatment of her mental illness as well as coming to terms with the stigma that mental illness has. **Miranda** struggled with her health, fighting cancer, redefining friendships, and fighting to live. **Tayder** struggled with English, not because she can't speak it, but rather because she's the only one in her nuclear family who can. This puts a lot of pressure on her to navigate through life for herself, advocating along the way for both her own needs and those of her family. And finally we have **Amanda** who endured physical and emotional abuse by her mother and had to learn how to accept the situation and that "love" can come from other sources, too. In her case, this was her foster mom.

The women featured here had something far more important, more meaningful than misfortunes. They had the resiliency to overcome these misfortunes, the desire to continue on, growing and changing at every turn, becoming the women they are today. The quality of resiliency cannot be underestimated. According to The Department of State,

"Resilience isn't about 'toughing it out' or reacting to every setback with a smile. Resilient people still feel sad, angry, or frustrated when faced with a setback. But they find ways to move forward, to tackle challenges with creativity, hope, and a positive attitude" [Bureau of Public Affairs].

We see in Amanda's story that she clearly possesses this quality or she wouldn't be where she is today. She endured emotional and sometimes physical abuse; however, she did have the support of a foster mom. According to Masten, Best, and Garmezy,

"children who experience chronic adversity fare better or recover more successfully when they have a positive relationship with a competent adult, they are good learners and problem-solvers, they are engaging to other people, and they have areas of competence and perceived efficacy valued by self or society" (2008).

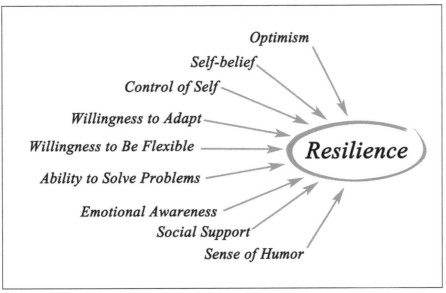

© arka38/Shutterstock.com

The question you might grapple with is, "How can I get resiliency? Is it a choice? Are we born with it? Is it something I can buy at the Dollar General?" It's more complicated than that and it requires us to dissect some of the aspects of resiliency and we'll start by looking at two important sub-components of resiliency: assets and resources.

According to an article titled, *Resiliency Theory: A Strengths-Based Approach to Research and Practice for Adolescent Health,* the most important factors in youth resiliency are what are referred to as assets and resources. Assets would include things like self-efficacy or self-esteem and resources would include a parental support system (Fergus-Zimmerman, 2005). Albert Bandura coined the term "self-efficacy" to mean, one's belief in one's ability to succeed in specific situations or accomplish a task (Bandura, 1977). Since Bandura's original work, efficacy has been studied on many levels, in varying facets and related to a large scope of issues from student motivation to mental health risk factors to performance outcomes. In short, the higher one's self-efficacy, the more resilient they should be. Self-efficacy is an asset that all of our young women in *Your Story Matters* have.

Zimmerman refers to **resources** in the realm of parental guidance, adult mentors, and even youth programs that work to build the confidence and capabilities of youth (2013). In each of the cases of our young women, they had both assets within themselves as well as resources that contributed to their abilities to get through the situations that they were put in or the circumstances they endured. Think about the external resources that helped or supported each of them. Sometimes it was a parent, but in other cases, it was a staff of nurses on the oncology floor, a foster mom, or a public health nurse. It proves the point that even if we don't find support within our inner sphere, there are still good people out there that will help us if we take the risk.

It is true, we cannot buy self-efficacy or resilience at the Dollar General and it's debatable whether it comes from our genes (nature) or our environment (nurture). Scientists still bicker over which one of these is more prominent in the human condition. It isn't as far of a reach as we imagine. I contend that it's in the middle and that we can build resiliency by improving our self-efficacy and also by expanding our resources. In addition, we need to work to become more skilled at managing stressors and coping with the travesties that come our way.

REFLECTION QUESTIONS

1. What is one example, in your life, where you have been resilient? Be specific, give examples.

2. What internal (within yourself) and external assets did you have that were partially responsible for this resiliency?

3. Where in your life do you have room to grow as it relates to resiliency?

REFERENCES

The Office of Website Management, The Bureau of Public Affairs. Retrieved from https://www.state.gov/m/med/dsmp/c44950.htm.

https://www.uky.edu/~eushe2/Bandura/Bandura1977PR.pdf

Fergus, S., & Zimmerman, M. A. (2005). Adolescent resilience: A framework for understanding healthy development in the face of risk. *Annual Review Public Health*, 26, 399–419.

Masten, A., Best, K., & Garmezy, N. (2008). Resilience and development: Contributions from the study of children who overcome adversity. *Development and Psychopathology*, 2(4), 425–444. doi:10.1017/S0954579400005812

https://www.psychologytoday.com/basics/resilience

https://www.psychologytoday.com/blog/fulfillment-any-age/201703/mistakes-dont-have-be-setbacks-3-ways-be-resilient

CPSIA information can be obtained
at www.ICGtesting.com
Printed in the USA
LVHW01s1212141217
559490LV00002B/3/P